Table of Contents

What's Wrong?

The shoes in only one of these pairs are perfectly matched. Can you tell what's wrong with the other pairs?

What's the Glitch?

Here is a page from the lost notebook of Leonardo's little-known second cousin, Herbie DaVinci. Read Herbie's notes and see if you can tell why this clever contraption might *not* be a great way to make tracks on the ocean floor.

Special Features of the Underwater Bi-sea-cle
- Ⓐ Studded Tires to grip ocean floor
- Ⓑ Air Supply for rider's convenience
- Ⓒ Pedals with Straps to hold feet in place
- Ⓓ Lightweight Tin Frame for tough underwater conditions
- Ⓔ Rubber Handles for better control

So ... What's The Glitch?

M. Nadel

What's Wrong with this Menu?

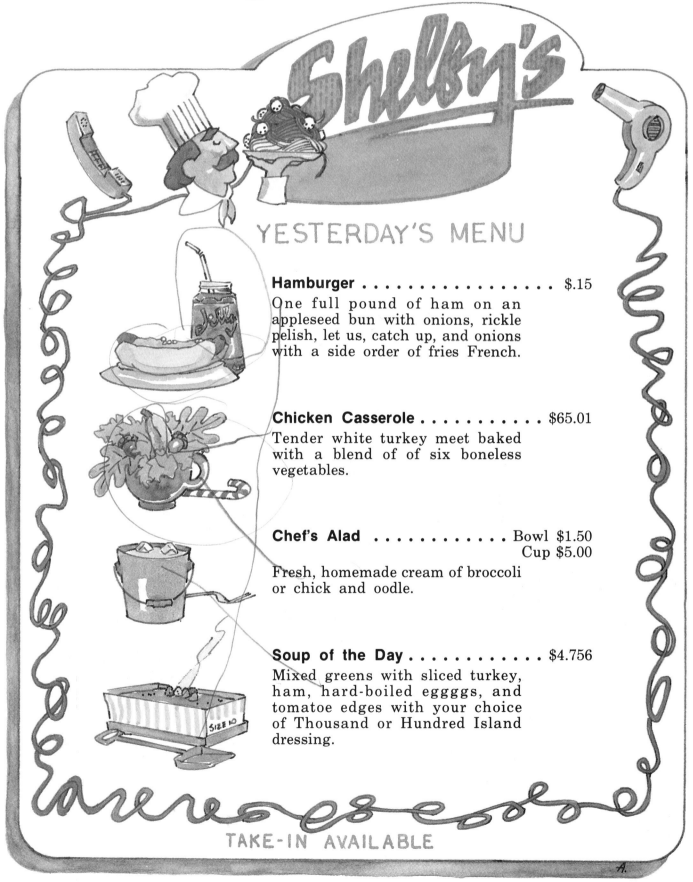

Shelby's

YESTERDAY'S MENU

Hamburger . . . . $.15
One full pound of ham on an appleseed bun with onions, rickle pelish, let us, catch up, and onions with a side order of fries French.

Chicken Casserole $65.01
Tender white turkey meet baked with a blend of of six boneless vegetables.

Chef's Alad . . . . Bowl $1.50
Cup $5.00
Fresh, homemade cream of broccoli or chick and oodle.

Soup of the Day $4.756
Mixed greens with sliced turkey, ham, hard-boiled eggggs, and tomatoe edges with your choice of Thousand or Hundred Island dressing.

TAKE-IN AVAILABLE

4

WHAT RHYMES?

We've replaced eight animals with pictures of words that rhyme with them. For example, where you might expect to see a cat, you'll find a hat. What other rhymes can you find?

1.

2.

3.

4.

5.

6.

Answers on page 158

What's Wrong?

What Do You Know About...?

1. Soccer players use their feet, legs, heads, and torsos to move the ball forward, but only one player is allowed to grasp the ball with the hands. Which player is it?
   A. striker
   B. goalie
   C. handyman
   D. forward

2. Every four years, the world's best soccer teams gather to compete in a tournament. The winner earns the...
   A. World Cup.
   B. Gold Medal.
   C. Stanley Cup.
   D. Academy Award.

3. In most countries other than the United States, soccer is known as...
   A. rugby.
   B. kickball.
   C. field hockey.
   D. football.

4. A score in soccer is called a...
   A. touchdown.
   B. goal.
   C. basket.
   D. bull's-eye.

5. Which of these is not an important soccer skill?
   A. dribbling
   B. passing
   C. marking
   D. hurdling

WHO'S WHO?

Susan, Craig, and Philip are all soccer players. From the clues below, can you tell who plays on which team? The team names are the Jets, the Hawks, and the Panthers.

1. No one's team name and first name begin with the same letter.
2. There are no girls on the Panthers this year.
3. Susan's team does not have an animal name.

Answers on page 158

What Happened?

Make up your own story to go with this picture.

What's Wrong?

WHAT AM I?

The animal answer to each of these riddles begins with the letter *P*. How many can you guess?

1. I shoot through the water like a torpedo
   Wearing a black and white tuxedo.
   What am I?

2. Close to me don't ever crouch.
   If you touch me, you will yell, "Ouch!"
   What am I?

3. I'm a mystery to science as well as a thrill
   With my animal's body and duck's feet and bill.
   What am I?

4. I may look like a giant, playful bear,
   Black, white, and cuddly, but beware!
   What am I?

5. My feathers have brightened rain forests for ages.
   Some of my small cousins live here in cages.
   What am I?

6. Unless you follow my earthen trail,
   You'll never catch me by the tail!
   What am I?

7. Although I swim with amazing ease,
   Don't confuse me with fishes, please.
   What am I?

8. With an ebony coat and a throaty growl,
   I'm sleek and quiet on the prowl.
   What am I?

Answers on page 158

What's Different?

There are at least 8 differences between these two pictures. How many can you find?

What's So Funny?

1. What do police fish travel in?

2. What do you call a rabbit who cuts the lawn?

3. What do you call a sleep-over for little oaks?

4. What kind of car would a kitten drive?

Answers on page 158

WHAT'S WRONG with these Pictures?

What's Wrong ?

WHAT'S NEXT?

Choose either A or B from the right to complete each numbered set of shapes on the left.

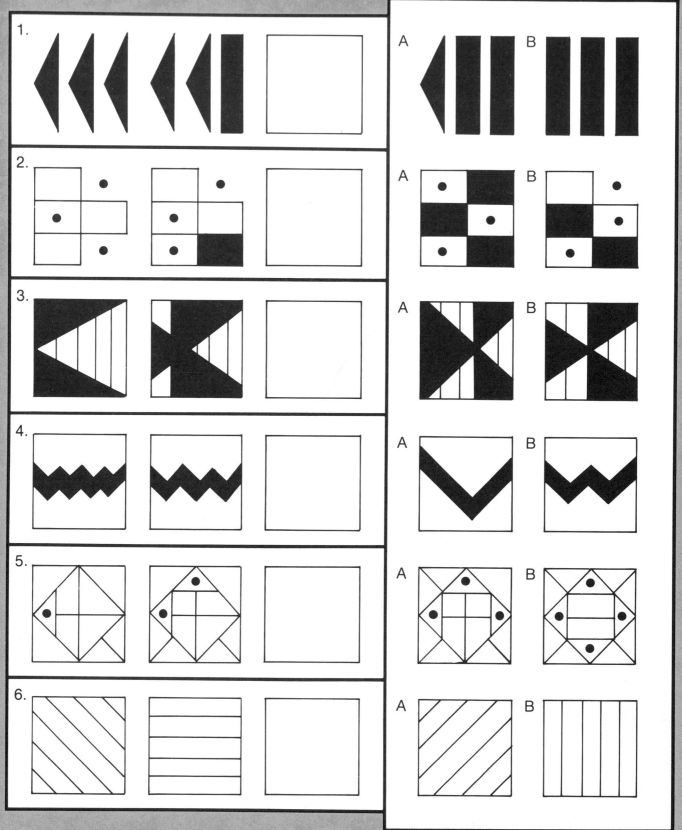

Answers on page 158

What's Wrong?

Hickory Dickory Dock

Hickory, dickory, dock,
The mouse ran up the clock.
The clock struck one,
The mouse ran down,
Hickory, dickory, dock.

What's Wrong?

What Do You Know About…?

1. If you were a gibbon, you would most likely be . . .
   A. building a nest in an evergreen in Maine.
   B. swinging from a vine in Asia.
   C. sliding on ice in Greenland.

2. If you were a termite, you would most likely be . . .
   A. digging a hole to bury a bone.
   B. spinning a cocoon in autumn.
   C. munching on a hardwood floor in springtime.

3. If you were a tapir, you would most likely be . . .
   A. eating South American plants.
   B. hunting beetles in the Florida Everglades.
   C. sliding down snowy hills in Siberia.

4. If you were a spoonbill, you would most likely be . . .
   A. dishing out ice cream in the Arctic.
   B. migrating to Canada for the winter.
   C. wading in warm water in Florida.

5. If you were a chameleon, you would most likely be . . .
   A. turning different colors to protect yourself from enemies.
   B. galloping across the western U.S. plains.
   C. flying in the Mexican moonlight.

6. If you were a skate, you would most likely be . . .
   A. singing from forest treetops.
   B. gliding along the ocean floor.
   C. sunning on a desert boulder.

Answers on page 158

WHAT'S WRONG?

Read the story and look at the picture. How many mistakes can you find?

Friday, June 12, was Aaron's tenth birthday. His Uncle Stephen and Aunt Celia gave him a book of mystery stories. His sister gave him a Chicago Cubs baseball cap. His mother gave him a green sweater with stripes, and new ice skates. They celebrated his birthday by playing miniature golf in the hot sun. Aaron said it was the best birthday he had had since he was twelve.

20

What's Alike?

Can you find 8 things that look the same in both of these pictures?

What's Wrong?

WHAT'S UP?

Sean fell asleep reading *Rip Van Winkle.* When he woke up, he couldn't remember what month it was. See if you can figure it out by searching the picture below for clues.

Answers on page 158

What's the Mix-Up?

Some of the letters in this story are mixed up. See if you can put them in the right places so the story makes sense. For an extra challenge, try reading the mixed-up story out loud . . . without laughing.

Terry and Julie wanted to ride their pikes to the bark on Maturday sorning. When they opened the darage goor, they realized it was haining very rard.

"Now what dill we wo?" asked Terry.

"Let's lake a mist of ideas and then ask Mom to bote for the vest one. That will delp us hecide what to do."

They lorked on their wist for a tong lime. Then they mave it to their gother. This is what it said:

Pake mopcorn
Bead rooks
Glay pames
Put on a suppet phow
Risten to lecords

"Which idea do you bike lest?" asked Julie.

"These are all fery vine ideas," said their mother, "but I shink you thould go for a ricycle bide."

They wooked out the lindow. Instead of sain they saw runshine! So off they pode to the rark just as they had planned.

WHAT IS IT?

Each picture below is a closeup look at part of a common object. Can you tell what each is?

1.

2.
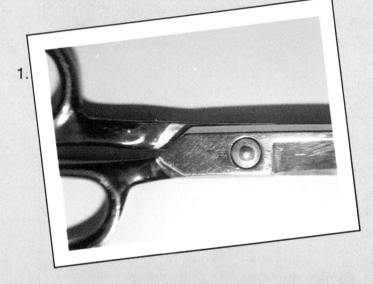

3.

4.
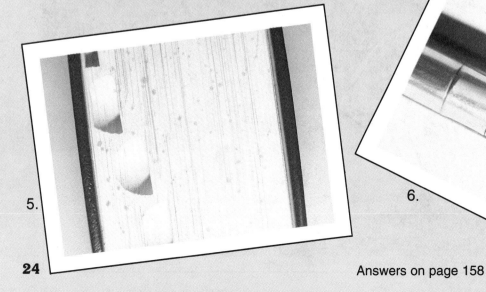

5.

6.

24   Answers on page 158

What's Wrong?

What's the Meaning of This?

Sometimes people say one thing when they mean another. See if you can guess the real meaning of each phrase below.

1. If you are told to **"take it with a grain of salt,"** you should . . .
   A. sprinkle salt on the sidewalk to make the ice melt.
   B. not take what's said too seriously.
   C. put salt on your food.

2. If she's **"egging her brother on,"** she's probably . . .
   A. urging him to do something.
   B. smearing egg on his plate.
   C. putting all her eggs in his basket.

3. **"The big cheese"** is . . .
   A. a big smile for a photographer.
   B. the largest plain pizza.
   C. a very important person.

4. If your sister **"spilled the beans,"** she . . .
   A. dropped a pot of bean soup on the floor.
   B. helped you preserve all the beans in the garden.
   C. accidentally told others a secret.

5. **"He's the cream of the crop,"** means . . .
   A. he likes ice cream a lot.
   B. he's the best.
   C. his hair is smooth and thick.

6. If something is **"as easy as pie,"** it is probably . . .
   A. very simple.
   B. apple flavored.
   C. covered with a crust.

Answers on page 158

What's Different?

There are at least 20 differences between these two pictures. How many can you find?

What's Your Number?

A. How many triangles can you find in the figure below?

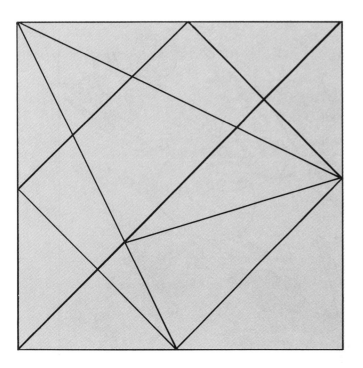

B. Complete the squares below so that the sums across, down, and diagonally are all the same.

?	2	?
4	6	8
5	10	?

C. In this series, what number comes next?

1   4   7   10   13   16   ?

D. Which stack of coins has the higher value?

1.

2.

28

Answers on page 158

What's Different?

There are at least 10 differences between these two pictures. How many can you find?

What's Wrong?

What's the Big Idea?

What do all these things have in common?

Answers on page 158

What's the Word?

What common word or phrase does each picture represent?

2. stand / i

1. USA MADE

4. PIGS PIGS PIGS

5. ever ever ever ever

6. B BOARD U L E T

7. MOVIE D R E

8. SIM says

9. SKY ____

10. AN na na na na na na na na na

11. FAST FAST

BREAD

What's Different?

There are at least 18 differences between these two pictures. How many can you find?

What's Different?

There are at least 20 differences between these two pictures. How many can you find?

What's Wrong?

What's the Glitch?

Here is a page from the lost notebook of Leonardo's little-known second cousin, Herbie DaVinci. Read Herbie's notes and see if you can tell why this clever contraption might *not* be a great way to keep your ears toasty warm.

SPECIAL FEATURES OF EAR MUFFINS
Cold Weather Headgear, Tasty Nutritious Snacks in One! Adjustable headband varies in length, keeping warm, freshly baked muffins snugly against ears. Muffins are stored within easy reach-No more tiresome trips to the kitchen!

So... What's the Glitch?

(Marc Nadel)

Answers on page 158

What's Wrong?

Read the story and look at the picture. How many things can you find wrong?

One cloudy day the moon was shining. A little girl named George was playing tag all alone in her backyard after school. Her brown dog, Snowflake, began meowing. She went to see what he was barking about, and she saw a rabbit up in a celery tree. She threw a rope to it. The rabbit climbed down the rope to safety.

The sun was beginning to come up, so the little girl finally went outside. Her mother was in the kitchen baking a tossed salad for dessert. Her father was in the kitchen, too, stirring some potato sandwiches. After she set the table for dinner, she turned the radio off and watched it until lunch was ready.

What Goes With What?

Match each numbered word with the name of the shape that goes with it. First you'll have to unscramble the names of the shapes!

1. Arctic   BUCE

2. Egyptian   ECON

3. Telephone   NILE

4. Ice   CLERIC

5. Baseball   QUESAR

6. Times   NOMADID

7. Bermuda   YAMDRIP

8. Ice-cream   NITRALEG

Answers on page 158

What Do You Know About ...?

TENNIS

1. You might be happy to have this on Valentine's Day, but in tennis it's something to avoid.
   - A. Heart
   - B. Card
   - D. Candy
   - C. Love

2. Waiters and tennis players spend a lot of time doing this.
   - A. Eating
   - B. Serving
   - C. Pouring
   - D. Talking

3. The tennis court is divided in half by this.
   - A. Wall
   - B. Net
   - C. Moat
   - D. Racket

4. A tennis match is won by the player who has taken the most . . .
   - A. sets
   - B. volleys
   - C. lobs
   - D. balls

5. This mistake would cost you a point.
   - A. Blunder
   - B. Balk
   - C. Gutter ball
   - D. Double fault

What's the Score?

Use the clues below to tell who won the most games at the tennis tournament. How many games did each of the other girls win?

Kari won twice as many games as Trina.

Brenda won five more games than Trina.

Sandy won half as many games as Trina.

No one won more than ten games or fewer than two.

What Happened?

Make up your own story to go with this picture.

What's Wrong?

41

WHAT AM I?

1. My first letter is in **eagle** twice.

2. My second letter is in **vest** but not **best**.

3. My third letter is in **tree** and **knee**.

4. My fourth letter is in **reach** but not **teach**.

5. My fifth letter is in **care** but not **car**.

6. My sixth letter is in **saw** but not **paw**.

7. My seventh letter is in **ten** but not **hen**.

I am the highest mountain peak in the world, located in the Himalayas on the Tibet-Nepal border. I am over 29,000 feet high.

Answers on page 158

What's Different?

There are at least 8 differences between these two pictures. How many can you find?

What's So Funny?

1. What veggie might you find in a chicken coop?

2. What did Pete Potato think of Carrie Carrot, and what did she think of him?

3. What veggie has the best rhythm?

4. What do the veggies say at harvest time?

Which Two Match?

Which bunny below is Binky, the twin of Ben Bunny above?

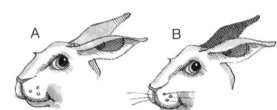

A   B

C   D

Answers on page 158

WHAT'S WRONG with these Pictures?

What's Wrong?

WHAT'S NEXT?

These pictures are out of order. For example, F happened first, G second and so forth. Can you figure out the logical order for the rest?

46

Answers on page 158

What's Wrong with Little Miss Muffet?

Little Miss Muffet
Sat on a tuffet
Eating her curds and whey;

Along came a spider
Who sat down beside her
And frightened Miss Muffet away.

49

What Do You Know About ...?

FOREIGN LANDS

Jennie Jetset went around the world so fast that she got a little mixed-up about what she did in each country. See if you can spot something wrong in each of her travel reports.

1. In China, I visited the Taj Mahal and the Great Wall and watched chefs cooking with woks.

2. In Brazil, I danced the samba, explored the Amazon, and spoke Spanish.

3. In Tanzania, I photographed wild animals on the Serengeti Plain and went boating on the Danube River.

4. In Norway, I visited the fjords, ate lots of the Norwegian national dish, lasagna, and enjoyed a stay in Oslo.

5. In Switzerland, I climbed in the Alps, ate chunks of cheese, and often sailed on the ocean.

6. In Puerto Rico, I used United States dollars, frolicked in the Caribbean Sea, and danced the traditional mazurka with the natives.

Answers on page 158

WHAT'S WRONG?

Read the story and look at the picture. How many mistakes can you find?

I'm glad I have my own room. I love my purple bedspread and my pink pillows. I like having a window so I can look out at our big old oak tree. I keep my stuffed panda and my red-haired doll on top of the toy chest at the head of my bed. My books are on my desk between two bookends that look like seashells. On my wall there's a picture of my great-grandmother when she was my age. Hanging from the ceiling is a mobile of birds. I love my room. Here is a picture of it.

What's Alike?

The shape of the banjo in the top picture is similar to the shape of the clock in the bottom picture. How many other similarities can you find?

What's Wrong?

WHAT'S UP?

Can you tell what Lizzie's job is just by looking at the clues in the picture below?

Answers on page 158

WHAT RHYMES?

Replace each circled word with a word that rhymes so that this report makes sense.

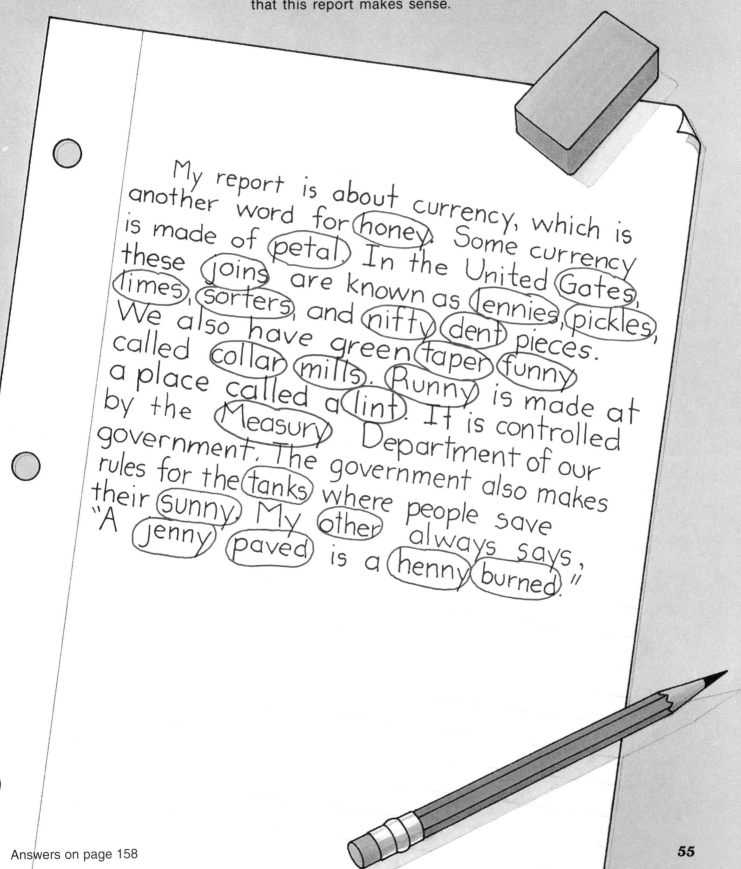

My report is about currency, which is another word for (honey). Some currency is made of (petal). In the United (Gates), these (joins) are known as (lennies), (pickles), (limes), (sorters), and (nifty) (dent) pieces. We also have green (taper) (funny) called (collar) (mills). (Runny) is made at a place called a (lint). It is controlled by the (Measury) Department of our government. The government also makes rules for the (tanks) where people save their (sunny). My (other) always says, "A (jenny) (paved) is a (henny) (burned)."

WHAT IS IT?

Here are the shapes of some common objects that have been made into strange animals. Can you identify the objects?

1.

2.

3.

4.

5.

6.

7.

8.

Answers on page 159

What's Different?

There are at least 10 differences between these two pictures. How many can you find?

What's the Meaning of This?

Sometimes people say one thing when they mean another. See if you can guess the real meaning of each saying below.

1. You say to your friend, "**Don't cry over spilled milk.**" You mean . . .

   A. her tears will make the milk on the floor salty.

   B. it's too late to worry about a mistake she made.

   C. she shouldn't slice onions with a glass of milk nearby.

2. If your mom "**brings home the bacon,**" she . . .

   A. leads a pig home on a leash.

   B. comes home from the grocery store.

   C. earns money for the household.

3. If someone "**butters you up,**" he . . .

   A. acts extra-nice to try to get something from you.

   B. spreads butter all over your clothing.

   C. puts your butter on the top shelf of the refrigerator.

4. When you "**upset the apple cart,**" you . . .

   A. spill a bushel of apples in the orchard.

   B. make a truck driver very angry.

   C. spoil plans by causing confusion.

5. "**That's a tough nut to crack**" means . . .

   A. that task is difficult to get done.

   B. the coconut is too green to open.

   C. your family doesn't have a nutcracker.

6. If someone tells you not to "**burn the midnight oil,**" she means . . .

   A. don't heat your house during the night.

   B. don't work too late.

   C. don't use vegetable oil in cooking.

Answers on page 159

What's Wrong?

What's Your Number?

Your Lucky Number

A. Take the number of planets in the Solar System Add the number of days in two years and two weeks. Add the number of pennies in a dollar minus three dimes. Subtract the number of continents. Multiply by the number of turtledoves "my true love gave to me" in the song. Add the number of moons the Earth has. Subtract the number of quarts in a half-gallon of mint chocolate chip ice cream. Add the number of minutes in sixty seconds. Divide by the number of white horses she'll be driving when "she's comin' round the mountain" in the song. Add the number of leaves in an ordinary clover, and you'll come up with the beginning of your lucky number! To make it yours alone, add your phone number, subtract your address, and multiply by your age.

Confuzzled Figures

B. Cal Q. Lator got confuzzled when he wrote this down! Which two figures have to switch places to make the correct answer 2151?

$$713$$
$$485$$
$$+962$$
$$\overline{}$$
$$2151$$

Apple Pickers

C. This tree had 106 crisp apples on it. Abby, Andy, Artie, and Zeb each picked the same number of apples from it. They picked all the apples except for ten that they couldn't reach at the top of the tree. How many apples did each person pick?

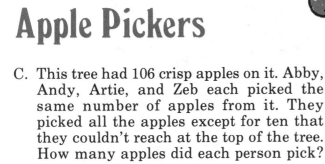

Answers on page 159

What's Different?

There are at least 8 differences between these two pictures. How many can you find?

61

What's the Big Idea?

What do all these things have in common?

Answers on page 159

What's the Word?

What common word or phrase does each picture represent?

1.

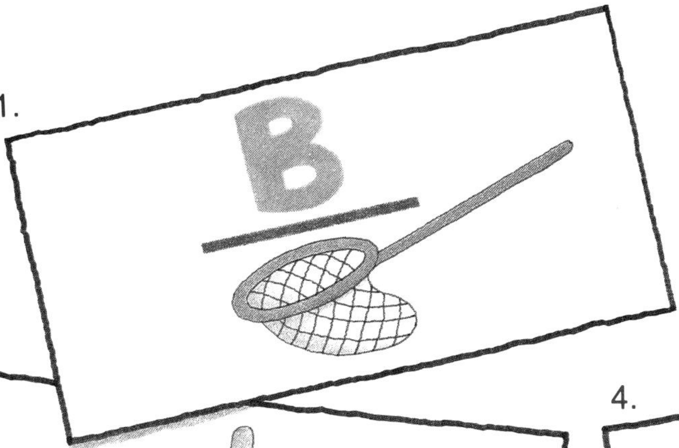
B

2.

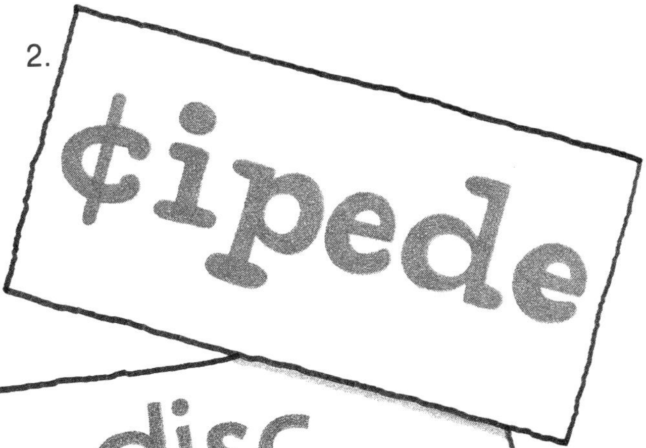
¢ipede

3.

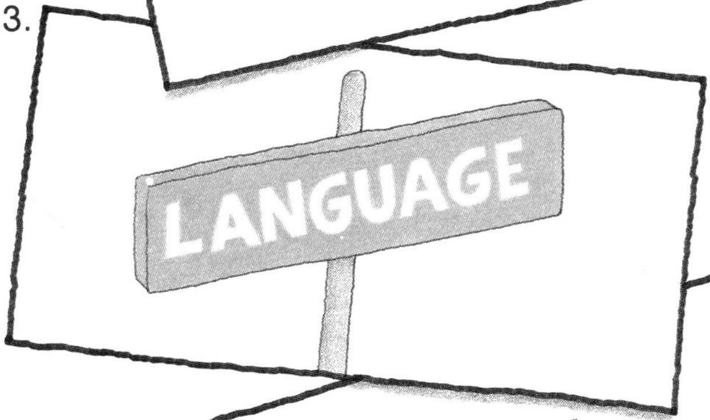
LANGUAGE

4.

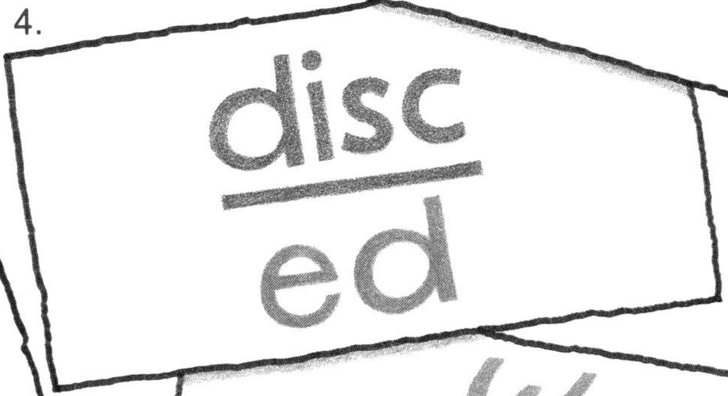
disc
ed

5.

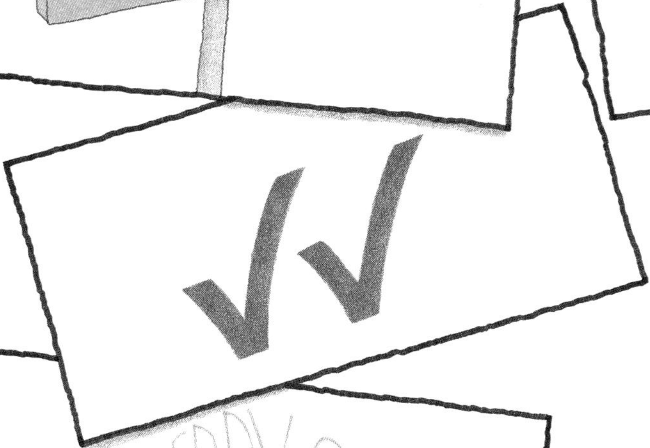

6.

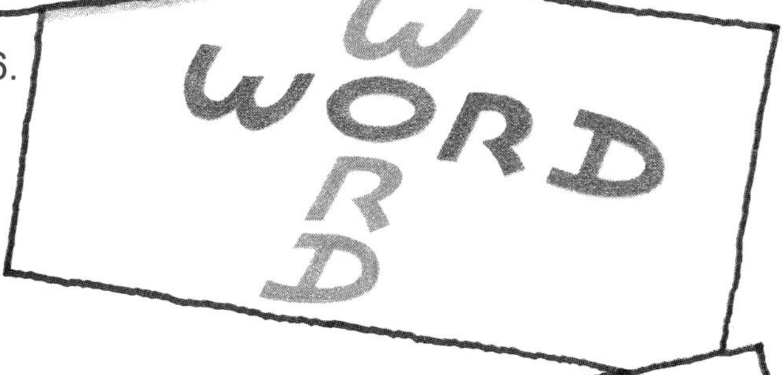
WORD
WORD

7.

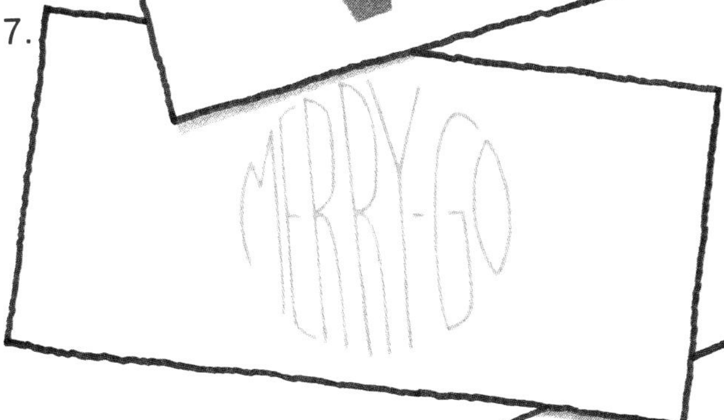
MERRY-GO

8.

egg
egg
easy

9.

TOUCH
KEEP

10.

LEFT
FOOD

Answers on page 159

What's Wrong?

Over the years
some things were saved in this button collection
that really don't belong.
Look closely to see how many you can find.

What's Different?

There are at least 10 differences between these two pictures. How many can you find?

What's Wrong?

What's the Glitch?

Here is a page from the lost notebook of Leonardo's little-known second cousin, Herbie DaVinci. Read Herbie's notes and see if you can tell why this clever contraption might not be a great way to explore the world.

SPECIAL FEATURES OF THE SUBMAR-OON~ At last! A handy, underwater, above land, through-the-air vehicle! Note periscope on <u>bottom</u> of sub. With hot air balloon inflated, periscope allows normal view just above ocean surface. Deflate balloon, and sub drops underwater, so periscope skims ocean floor, offering easy viewing of sunken treasure.

So...What's the Glitch?

Answers on page 159

What's Wrong with these Want Ads?

Want-Ads

Advertise with us
Free
Only 10¢ per letter

We will sell your merchandise or it's yours to keep!

House for Sale: Ranch-style, roofless high-rise in Phoenix, Wyoming. Three bedrooms—two upstairs, two downstairs. Updated basement with enclosed patio on third floor. Ten-car garage features coal-burning fireplace and Dutch oven doors. No pets, please. Spectacular ocean view.

Antiques for Sale: Rare World War I photographs of Vice-Presidents Franklin and Washington at their first live radio broadcast from the White House, microwave oven, large collection of CD's from early 40s, assortment of prehistoric men's neckless shirts (size 6), one pair of mahogany oak canopy bunk beds (queen size).

Babysitter Wanted: Permanent, full-time, live-in care for my three infant twins, ages 2, 5, 7, and 19. Shorthand and some calculus required. Irresponsible kindergartener or irate Sophomore Citizen preferred. My home or yours. Maximum of three hours per week.

Lawn Service Offered: Three strong, lazy, two-year-old teenagers will mow and wax your lawn, driveway, pool, or flower garden weekly every morning after school for just $8 per minute. We both have mediocre references and no experience necessary. You provide the shovels, we provide the chain saws. Available Sept. 31 threw Feb. 30.

Help Wanted: Dental hygienist needed from noon to midnight 8 days a week to greet vegetables and answer doorbell at new supermarket opening soon in your home. Choose your own hours. Good starting celery and few benefits. Bowling shoes and out-of-date driver's license required, but not helpful. Excellent opportunity to work overtime at one-tenth your normal wages during our busy Christmas season.

Motorcycle for Sale: Too-door convertible with for-wheel drive and no steering. Brand new—never worn. Fair condition. Needs new spokes and pedals. Only 80,000 miles. Central air conditioning. $30 firm. Will take best offer.

What's the Right Way Home?

When Cara visits her friend Tina, she goes down two flights of stairs, out her front door, faces east and walks one-half block to the corner. She crosses the street and walks two more blocks. Then she turns north and walks three blocks. She crosses the street, makes a right turn, and goes into the third building on her left. Tina lives on the second floor. If Cara wants to go home by exactly the same route, which of the following should she do?

1. Walk down two flights of steps. Turn right and walk to the corner. Turn left, cross the street and walk three blocks. Cross the street, turn west and walk two and a half blocks. Enter her building through the front door and go down two flights of stairs.

2. Walk down one flight of steps. Turn right and walk to the corner. Turn left, cross the street and walk three blocks. Cross the street, turn west and walk two and a half blocks. Enter her building through the front door and go up two flights of stairs.

3. Walk down one flight of steps. Turn right and walk to the corner. Turn left, cross the street and walk two blocks. Cross the street, turn west and walk four blocks. Enter her building through the front door and go up one flight of stairs.

4. Walk down one flight of steps. Turn right and walk to the corner. Turn left, cross the street and walk three blocks. Cross the street, turn east and walk two and a half blocks. Enter her building through the front door and go up two flights of stairs.

Answers on page 159

What's Wrong?

What Do You Know About ...?

BICYCLING

1. Holding your left hand down with your palm facing back means . . .
   A. you want to pass another bicyclist.
   B. you are preparing to stop.
   C. you are waving at another bicyclist.

2. The most famous yearly cross-country bicycle race is called the . . .
   A. Tour De Detours.
   B. Tour De Eiffel.
   C. Tour De France.

3. The center of a wheel where the spokes come together is called the . . .
   A. hub.
   B. nub.
   C. hobnob.

4. Racing bikes often feature pedal attachments called . . .
   A. pedal pushers.
   B. stirrups.
   C. toe clips.

5. A bicycle's gears are attached to . . .
   A. the front wheel only.
   B. the rear wheel only.
   C. both wheels.

WHO WON?

Doug, Lauren, and Andrew took the top three prizes in a bicycle race. Use the clues to discover which of them finished first, second, and third, and what color bicycle each one rode.

Doug finished ahead of the orange bicycle only.

The yellow bicycle did not finish in first place.

Andrew was not riding the green bicycle.

Answers on page 159

What Happened?

Make up your own story to go with the picture.

What's Wrong ?

WHO AM I?

I'm one of nine.
I wear a glove.
I play a game
That Americans love.
 Who am I?

I kick and leap,
That's how I go.
I twirl and bend
While on my toe.
 Who am I?

I turn a wheel
While riding high.
I give a honk
While passing by.
 Who am I?

I rise up early
And off I go.
I'm on a roll.
I make the dough.
 Who am I?

I'll change for you
Whatever you say.
I handle green
And count all day.
 Who am I?

I make you smile.
I make you freeze.
And when I shoot,
I aim to please.
 Who am I?

Answers on page 159

What's Different?

There are at least 8 differences between these two pictures. How many can you find?

75

What's So Funny?

1. What kind of snake loves dessert?

2. What prize does the Olympic sneezing champion win?

3. What's the best month for a parade?

4. What do you call a prince's mother who's a golf pro?

Which One Isn't Right?

Can you find what's wrong with one of these six panels?

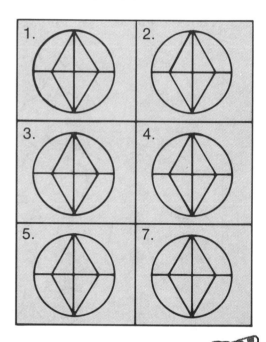

Answers on page 159

WHAT'S WRONG with these Pictures?

What's Wrong?

WHAT'S NEXT?

These pictures are out of order. For example, C happened first, F second, and so forth. Can you figure out the logical order for the rest?

Answers on page 159

What's Wrong?

Hey diddle, diddle,
The cat and the fiddle,
The cow jumped over the moon.
The little dog laughed to see such sport
And the dish ran away with the spoon.

What's Wrong?

R CLUBB HOU

PEANUT BUTTER

80

What Do You Know About...?

See if you can choose the correct name of each relative described in the clues below.

1. Your parents have three children. You are the youngest, the only girl. The two oldest children are your . . .
A. uncles.
B. brothers.
C. nephews.

2. Your mother's mother is your . . .
A. grandmother.
B. great-aunt.
C. great-grandmother.

3. Your brother's wife is your . . .
A. sister-in-law.
B. aunt.
C. second cousin.

4. Your father's brother is your . . .
A. cousin.
B. nephew.
C. uncle.

5. Your father's sister's daughter is your . . .
A. niece.
B. first cousin.
C. second cousin.

6. Your mother's brother's wife is your . . .
A. aunt.
B. great-aunt.
C. second cousin.

7. Your mother's mother's father is your . . .
A. great-uncle.
B. grandfather.
C. great-grandfather.

8. Your grandmother's sister is your . . .
A. cousin.
B. great-aunt.
C. aunt.

9. Your brother's son is your . . .
A. first cousin.
B. second cousin.
C. nephew.

10. Your sister's daughter's daughter is your . . .
A. grand niece.
B. niece.
C. great aunt.

Answers on page 159

WHAT'S WRONG
With This Slide Show?

Cameron wanted to show her vacation slides to her friends. She wrote notes to herself about each slide. When she began the show, it was too dark to see her notes, so she had to make up words as she went along. In her confusion she mixed up some of the details. By looking at the pictures can you straighten out her story?

1. Here we are at "Old Faithful."

2. We put on sneakers to go under the falls.

3. We went right over the falls!

4. Afterward we had pizza on the Canadian side.

5. Then we crossed over to the American side and ate fresh roasted peanuts.

6. Then we got back on the train and rode home.

What's Alike?

Can you find 8 things that look the same in both of these pictures?

What's Wrong ?

WHAT'S UP?

Barry's mother cooked hot dogs on the grill one Saturday afternoon. She put them on a plate and left them on the picnic table for a moment while she went to the kitchen for pickle relish. When she returned, the hot dogs had disappeared. Barry says he and his friends were busy playing volleyball and didn't see anyone come into the yard. Can you guess who hijacked the hot dogs?

Answers on page 159

What's Out of Place?

In each set of four things, which one doesn't belong? Why not?

1. cherries
   pumpkins
   oranges
   apples

2. Bo-Peep
   Jack Sprat
   Humpty Dumpty
   Ugly Duckling

3. San Antonio
   Dallas
   Albuquerque
   Austin

4. pedals
   saddle
   reins
   stirrups

5. zither
   accordion
   racquet
   trombone

6. apple
   pineapple
   ukulele
   luau

7. 12.5 x 4
   123 - 73
   18 + 12 + 3 + 12 + 5
   25 ÷ 2

8. zebra
   donkey
   macaw
   burro

9. George Washington
   Theodore Roosevelt
   Alexander Hamilton
   Gerald Ford

10. refrigerator
    dresser
    stove
    sink

11. guitar
    flute
    violin
    banjo

12. Seattle, Washington
    Dover, Delaware
    Carson City, Nevada
    Frankfort, Kentucky

WHAT IS IT?

Here are some words you may not hear very often. See if you can find the picture that goes with each one.

aglet   tripod
turret   cloak
chariot   trellis
shrubbery   finial
cask   gazebo

1.

2.

3.

4.

5.

6.

7.

8.

9.

10.

What's Different?

There are at least 8 differences between these two pictures. How many can you find?

MARTIN
FILCHOCK

What's the Meaning of This?

Sometimes people say one thing when they mean another. See if you can guess the real meaning of each phrase below.

1. If she's "**in a jam,**" she has probably . . .
A. spilled jelly all over the floor.
B. gotten herself into trouble.
C. caught her finger between the door and the molding.

2. If you are "**using your noodle,**" you are . . .
A. thinking.
B. hitting someone with wet spaghetti.
C. making a necklace out of macaroni.

3. "**Butter won't melt in your mouth**" means . . .
A. your mouth is cold.
B. your family uses margarine.
C. you behave politely, even though you don't feel that way inside.

4. If he "**packs a punch,**" he . . .
A. fills a punch bowl to the top.
B. hits hard.
C. puts boxing gloves in a suitcase.

5. If someone says, "**You take the cake,**" they may mean . . .
A. you are a bakery delivery person.
B. you bring the soap into the bathtub with you.
C. you are unbelievable!

6. If he's "**feeling his oats,**" he is probably . . .
A. touching his oatmeal to see if it's too hot.
B. feeling very brave and strong.
C. checking to see if the oat crop is ready to be harvested.

90

Answers on page 159

What's Wrong?

What's Your Number?

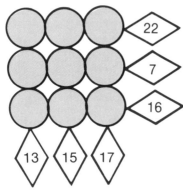

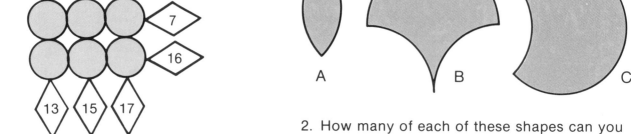

A   B   C

1. Which set of numbers below, when added across and down, will give you the sums shown in the diamonds?

2. How many of each of these shapes can you find in the figure below?

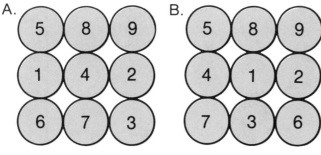

A.   B.

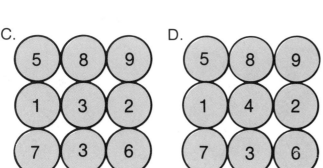

C.   D.

4. Ted's grandmother invited him to meet her downtown for lunch. Ted took the 10:05 train to the city and arrived at the station three-quarters of an hour later. It took him sixteen minutes to walk to his grandmother's office. He waited in the lobby for ten minutes. Then Ted and his grandmother spent half an hour touring the building and meeting the people who work there. They walked to a restaurant that was five minutes away. What time did Ted and his grandmother reach the restaurant?

3. Which picture correctly shows the measurements on one inch of a ruler?

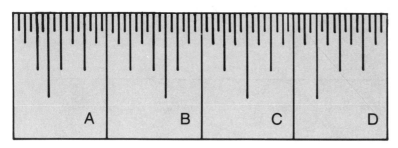

A   B   C   D

Answers on page 159

What's Different?

There are at least 10 differences between these two pictures. How many can you find?

What's the Big Idea?

What do these things have in common?

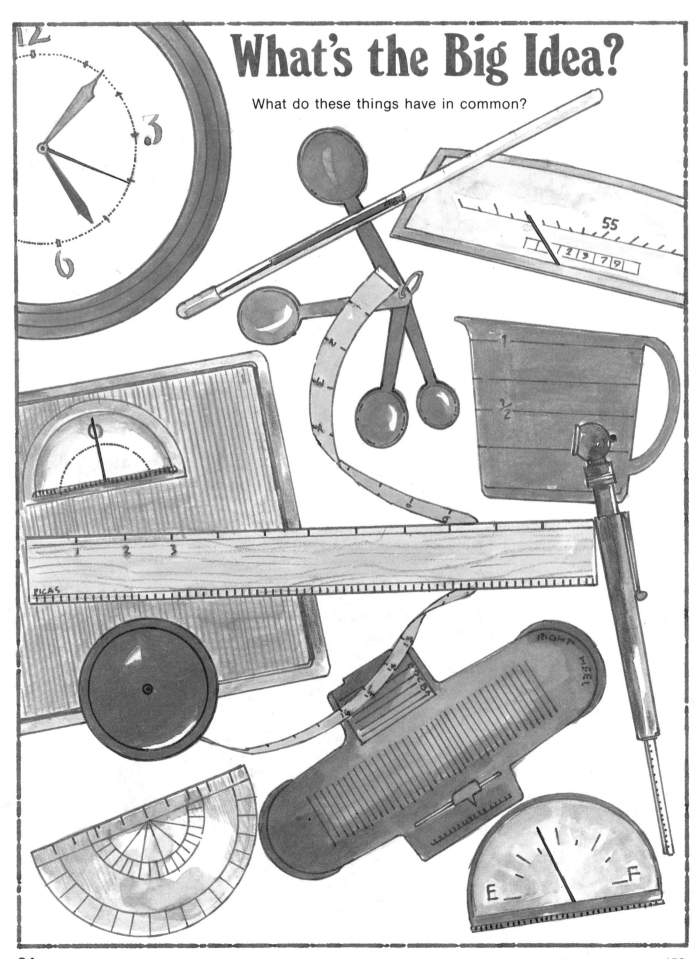

Answers on page 159

What's the Word?

What word or common phrase does each picture represent?

1.

nothing new

2. ESCAPE

3. 1 HOLE

4. LEM ADE

5. OFF

6. CALL

7. header header

8. 1 2 3 4 5

9. (coin) URY

10. BACK

Answers on page 159

What's Different?

There are at least 10 differences between these two pictures. How many can you find?

What's Different?

There are at least 15 differences between these two pictures. How many can you find?

What's Wrong?

What's the Glitch?

Here is a page from the lost notebook of Leonardo's little-known second cousin, Herbie DaVinci. Read Herbie's notes and see if you can tell why this clever contraption might not be a great way to top off your sandwich!

SPECIAL FEATURES of the JELLY-COPTER

Tired of waiting at the table while Mom prepares a nice, hot lunch for you? Does this stop you from doing something important, like playing with blocks? Then this device is for you! Jelly stored in body of copter squirts out of nozzles as they start spinning. Bread slices revolve in opposite direction, and quickly get covered with yummy goo. Remote-controlled flight of Jelly-copter delivers lunch to you ... lickety-split!

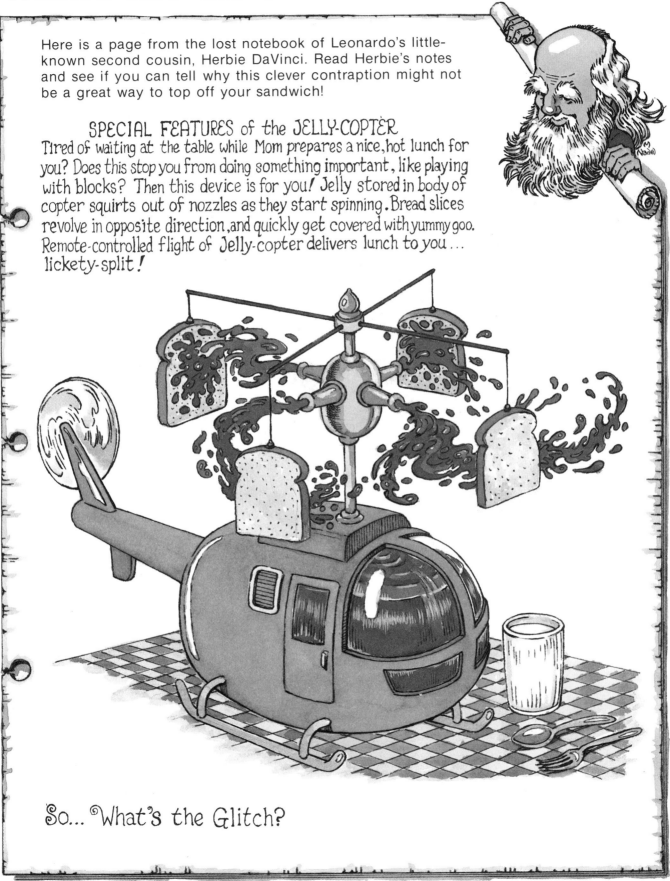

So... What's the Glitch?

Answers on page 159

What's Wrong with this Letter?

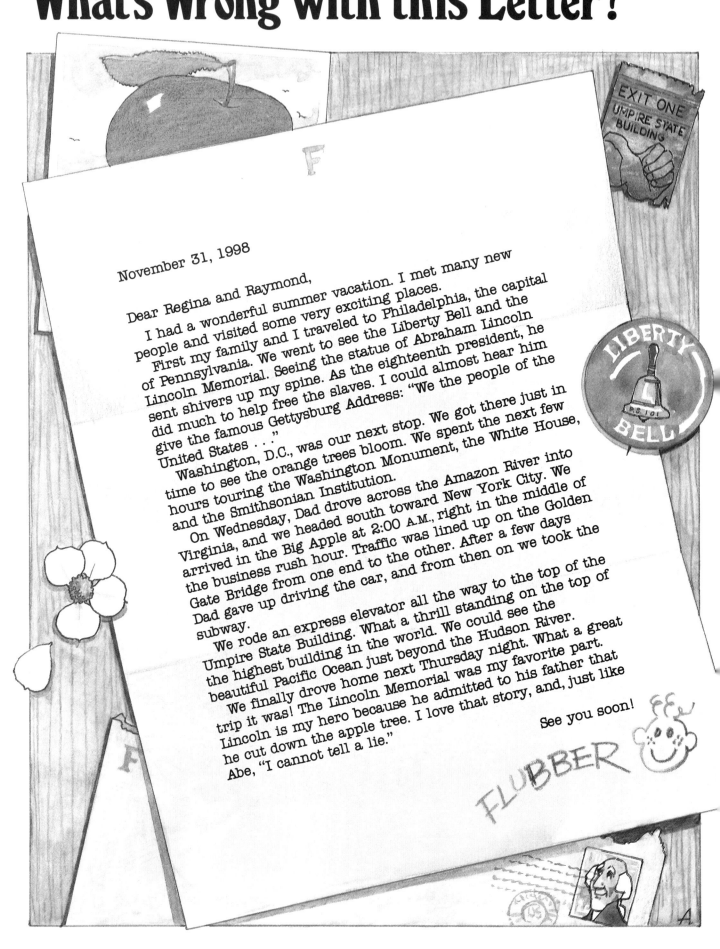

November 31, 1998

Dear Regina and Raymond,

I had a wonderful summer vacation. I met many new people and visited some very exciting places.

First my family and I traveled to Philadelphia, the capital of Pennsylvania. We went to see the Liberty Bell and the Lincoln Memorial. Seeing the statue of Abraham Lincoln sent shivers up my spine. As the eighteenth president, he did much to help free the slaves. I could almost hear him give the famous Gettysburg Address: "We the people of the United States . . ."

Washington, D.C., was our next stop. We got there just in time to see the orange trees bloom. We spent the next few hours touring the Washington Monument, the White House, and the Smithsonian Institution.

On Wednesday, Dad drove across the Amazon River into Virginia, and we headed south toward New York City. We arrived in the Big Apple at 2:00 A.M., right in the middle of the business rush hour. Traffic was lined up on the Golden Gate Bridge from one end to the other. After a few days Dad gave up driving the car, and from then on we took the subway.

We rode an express elevator all the way to the top of the Umpire State Building. What a thrill standing on the top of the highest building in the world. We could see the beautiful Pacific Ocean just beyond the Hudson River.

We finally drove home next Thursday night. What a great trip it was! The Lincoln Memorial was my favorite part. Lincoln is my hero because he admitted to his father that he cut down the apple tree. I love that story, and, just like Abe, "I cannot tell a lie."

See you soon!

FLUBBER

What's the Mix-Up?

One word is scrambled in each of these sentences. Please put the letters back in order so these silly sentences will make sense.

1. The large pea at the zoo frightened us.

2. The boy put the groceries in a paper gab.

3. Ida always puts a plum of sugar in her tea.

4. Jimmy says his dog is part flow.

5. I hurt my ram when I threw the ball.

6. Ed and I are members of the swimming meat.

7. Carol always walks at a fast cape.

8. The baby was taking a pan when we arrived.

9. I love to dear the story of Cinderella.

10. Mother asked Sarah not to plug her milk.

11. The bandleader bought a new bulge.

12. The beavers were busy building a mad.

Answers on page 159

What Do You Know About ...?

BASKETBALL

Choose the right description for each of the basketball rule violations named in this quiz.

1. If a player is traveling, she
   A. is taking more than one step with the ball, without dribbling.
   B. is going from town to town for league games.
   C. is visiting other countries to watch games and get ideas for her home team.

2. The dreaded double dribble occurs when
   A. twin players spill water down their chins at halftime.
   B. the player stops dribbling the ball and then starts again before another player touches it.
   C. a player stops dribbling the ball and lets another player touch it before he touches it again.

3. In palming the ball, the player
   A. places the ball in the fronds of a palm tree to deceive the other players.
   B. holds the ball in the palm of his hand before throwing it.
   C. uses the palm of his hand to control the ball when dribbling.

4. A technical foul results in
   A. the other team getting a free throw.
   B. the computerized scoreboard showing all zeros.
   C. chicken dinners for technical school team members.

Who Has the Ball?

Ned, Ted, Ed, Fred, and Sylvester are playing basketball. Use the clues below to tell who has the ball.

Ned and Fred are taller than Sylvester.

Ed has red hair.

Sylvester is wearing blue shorts.

Ted forgot his shorts and borrowed a pair from Ned.

Ted is closer to Fred than Ed is.

Answers on page 159

What Happened?

Make up your own story to go with the picture.

WHAT AM I?

1. I am green.

2. I can grow in the woods, around your yard, or in many other places.

3. I don't bother animals.

4. I do bother people who don't notice me.

5. You can recognize me by my leaves.

6. People use a lot of unpleasant words to describe me.

7. Sometimes people are "itchy" after being around me.

8. Sometimes people go to the doctor because of me.

9. My scrambled letters are V O S I P I O N Y.

Answers on page 159

What's Different?

There are at least 12 differences between these two pictures. How many can you find?

What's So Funny?

1. Why did the zebra think it could fly?

2. Why do spiders spin webs?

3. What's the best way to catch a squirrel?

4. Where do cows get their medicine?

Which Two Match?

How quickly can you find the two panels that match?

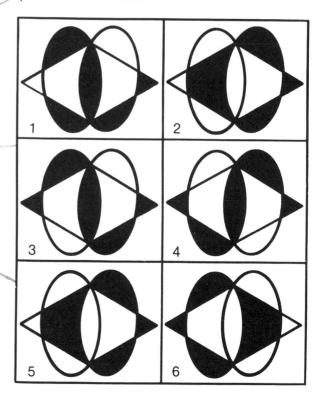

WHAT'S WRONG with these Pictures?

PUSH TO OPEN

BASSO

Answers on page 159

What's Different?

There are at least 8 differences between these two pictures. How many can you find?

WHAT'S NEXT?

Choose either A or B from the right to complete each numbered set of shapes on the left.

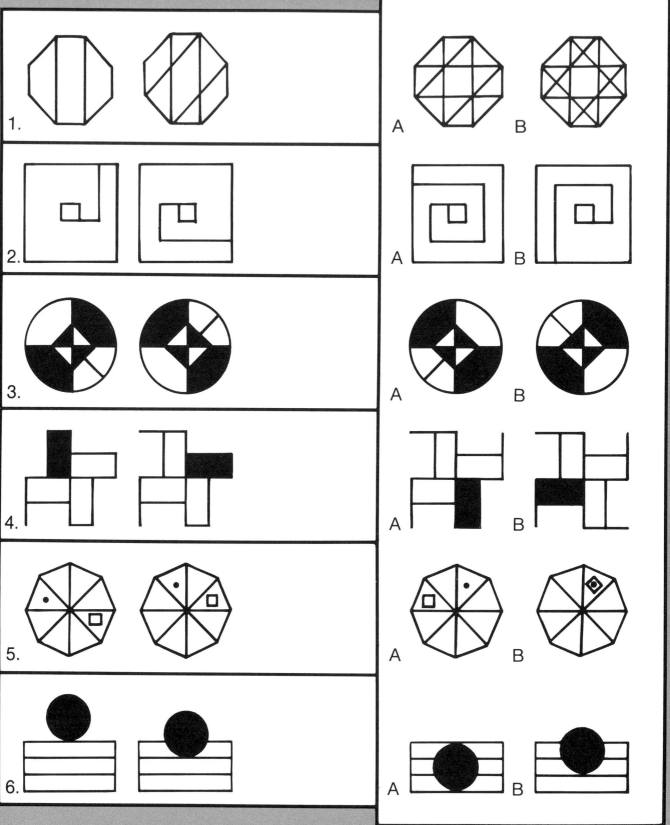

Answers on page 159

WHAT'S WRONG
with this Nursery Rhyme?

Little Boy Blue,
Comb blow your horn.
The sheep's on the medal,
The cow's on acorn.

Where's Little Boy Blue
Who looks after the sheep?
Under a . . . Hey! Stack
Faster! Leap!

M. Nadel

What Do You Know About ...?

1. The three states bordering California are:

   A. Oregon   C. Arizona
   B. Nebraska   D. Nevada

2. The five Great Lakes include:

   A. Huron   D. Victoria
   B. Superior   E. Erie
   C. Michigan   F. Ontario

3. Two states of the United States are separated from the rest. These include:

   A. Alaska   C. Hawaii
   B. New Mexico   D. Canada

4. There is only one place in the United States where four states touch. These four states are:

   A. Kansas   D. Utah
   B. New Mexico   E. Arizona
   C. Colorado

5. Five states touch the Pacific Ocean. These five states are:

   A. Alaska   D. Texas
   B. California   E. Washington
   C. Oregon   F. Hawaii

6. There are four states whose names begin with *New*. These are:

   A. New York   D. New Mexico
   B. New Rochelle   E. New Jersey
   C. New Hampshire

Answers on page 159

WHAT'S WRONG?

Read the story and look at the picture. What's wrong?

And here we have the monkeys, folks. Wearing the red jacket and eating a watermelon is Moko. And the monkey who's crying under the cucumber bush is Komey. Behind them is Bruno, the big polar bear. That bird with a green and red head is our robin. Notice the lion at the left—don't worry, this high chain-link fence will protect you. See the rhinoceros wading in the river! And notice the beautifully polka-dotted zebras, the red-and-white checked giraffes, and the bright-yellow elephants, begging for pizza as usual. Over there, looking as if they're wearing jeans and T-shirts, are the penguins. Well, it's midnight, so for now it's good-bye to the zoo.

What's Alike?

Can you find 8 things that look the same in both of these pictures?

What's Wrong?

WHAT'S UP?

A man claiming to be an astronaut who has walked on the moon is speaking to the people of Smithtown. You are an investigative reporter covering the speech. It is up to you to determine whether or not he is a real astronaut. Here is part of his speech. What can you tell from it?

"We landed on the Moon on July 20, 1969. We had traveled for four whole days to get there. The Moon is like another world. Everything is gray and white, and the ground is fine and powdery. The Moon has rocks, boulders, valleys, craters, and huge green plants unlike any we have on Earth. Sometimes it got so warm on the Moon that all five of us had to take off our space suits and rest. We drank from the mountain streams and found the water cool and refreshing. Exploring the Moon was really exciting, until our car ran out of gasoline. We had to walk for five hours to get back to the ship."

Answers on page 159

What's Wrong with this Tale?

Here are ten sentences about characters from familiar rhymes and stories. In each one, something is not quite right. See if you can change one word in each sentence to set the story straight.

1. There was an old woman who lived in a sock.
2. Little Miss Muffet sat on a buffet.
3. Cinderella lost her glove at the ball.
4. When Pinocchio told lies, his ears grew and grew.
5. Rapunzel hung her sash out of the tower so that the prince could climb up to her.
6. Everywhere that Mary went, her kitten was sure to go.
7. Snow White had nine friends who were dwarfs.
8. Dorothy went to see the Wizard of Oz, hoping he would help her get back to Ohio.
9. Sleeping Beauty awoke when the prince shook her.
10. A coyote dressed up as Little Red Riding Hood's grandmother.

Answers on page 160

WHAT IS IT?

Can you identify the common object in each picture?

2.

1.

3.

4.

5.

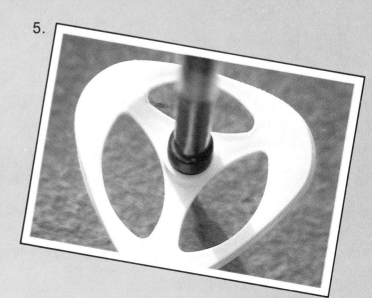

120

Answers on page 160

What's Different?

There are at least **10** differences between these two pictures. How many can you find?

What's the Meaning of This?

1. **"That's my cup of tea"** means . . .
   A. I don't like coffee.
   B. that is something I really like.
   C. my golf ball went from the tee to the cup in one shot.

2. **"He doesn't have a leg to stand on"** means . . .
   A. he swam too far out in the water.
   B. he has no basis for winning an argument.
   C. he has both legs in casts.

3. A card you receive is signed **"from the bottom of my heart."** It really says . . .
   A. "with my most sincere feelings."
   B. the bottom of someone's heart sent the message.
   C. the top of the sender's heart is missing.

4. If you've **"gotten yourself in a pickle,"** you've . . .
   A. found a pickle big enough to climb into.
   B. gotten yourself into trouble.
   C. walked into the middle of a cucumber patch.

5. If someone is **"making a pig of himself,"** he is . . .
   A. drawing a picture of a pig.
   B. dressing up for Halloween.
   C. eating too much.

6. If your sister has **"a bee in her bonnet,"** she . . .
   A. is obsessed with one idea.
   B. has put the letter **B** under her hat.
   C. has a barrette stuck in her hair.

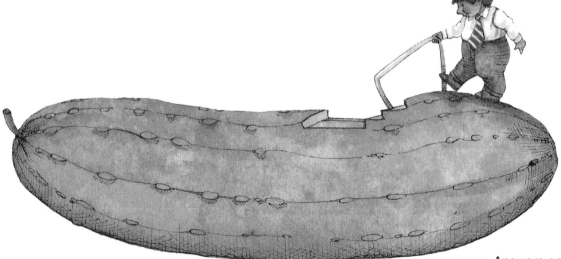

122

Answers on page 160

What's Wrong?

What's Your Number?

1. Which lemonade stand's special offer gives you the best price per glass?

2. How many circles are there in this figure?

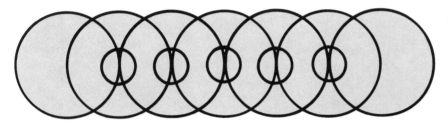

3. How many times will the minute hand of a clock be on top of the hour hand in one twenty-four-hour period that starts and ends at midnight?

4. How many of these pictures include a mistake?

124

Answers on page 160

What's Wrong?

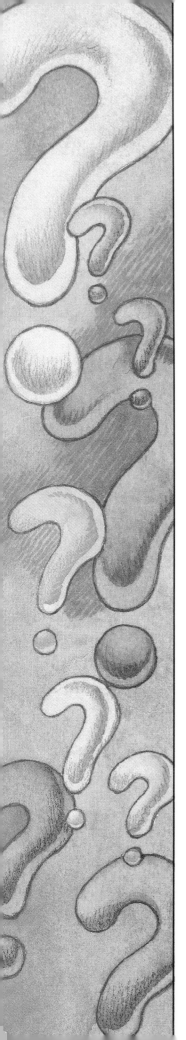
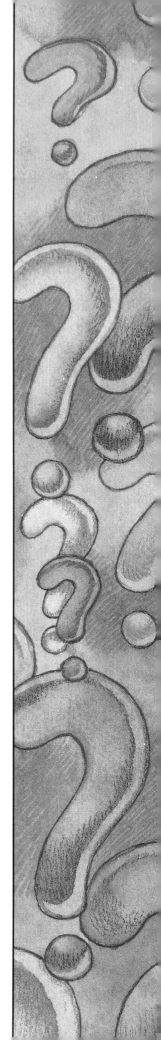

What's the Big Idea?

The three words in each set have something in common. Can you match each unlikely trio with the word that ties its members together?

1. Potato
   Needle
   Hurricane   A. Ball

2. River
   Dormitory
   Flower garden   B. Bar

3. Car
   Bull
   Tuba   C. Bed

4. Gum
   Beach
   Foot   D. Blade

5. Wedding
   Ear
   Doorbell   E. Card

6. High
   Lawn
   Rocking   F. Chair

7. Knife
   Grass
   Shoulder   G. Eye

8. Board
   Table
   Greeting   H. Horn

9. Paddle
   Chair
   Steering   I. Ring

10. Candy
    Monkey
    Salad   J. Wheel

Answers on page 160

What's the Word?

What animals do these pictures represent?

1.

2.

3.

4.

5.

6.

Answers on page 160

What's Different?

There are at least 15 differences between these two pictures. How many can you find?

What's Different?

There are at least 15 differences between these two pictures. How many can you find?

What's the Glitch?

Here is a page from the lost notebook of Leonardo's little-known second cousin, Herbie DaVinci. Read Herbie's notes and see if you can tell why this clever contraption might *not* be a great solution to your trouser troubles.

Special Features of Scrambled Legs : For those times when your suedes get soaked in a storm, or your gaberdines get grass stains, or you just muddle through one too many mud puddles, here's a solution for your trouser troubles! Scrambled Legs are four pairs of pants in one, each being attached to the others at the waist. When one pair gets dirty, a drawstring neatly pulls it up, folds it, and stores the bundle in its own individual backpack. Select a clean pair, and you're ready for another round of muddy fun!

So... What's the Glitch?

Answers on page 160

What's Odd About These Ads?

Takeoff Airlines

Take off with Takeoff! All amateur pilots—none over 18. Takeoff takes all the major interstate highways. Sometimes we get as much as six feet off the ground! All our planes have at least one wing. You'll be surprised at the places we land—we always are.

ARCHIE'S ARCHITECTS

Skycrapers from one to one hundred stories. Florida igloos our specialty! Architects fresh from leading kindergartens—all have diplomas in Block Stacking and Sandbox Sandscapes.

Against-the-Grain Bakery

Delicious bread, rolls, roofs, cakes, cars, and cooks!

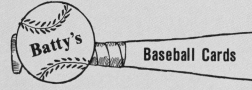

Batty's Baseball Cards

Collectors—we have all the great baseball players—Ty Cobb, Hank Aarons, Ben Franklin, Tom Jefferson, George Washington, Abe Lincoln, Ted Williams, Babe Ruth, Cal Coolidge.

Curly's Beauty Salon

Haircuts—Permanents—Temporaries—Walk in—We guarantee your friends will be stunned when you walk out.

Dizzy Dancin' School

Ballfield Dancing—Waltz, Foxgallop, Jitterinsect, Tap, Knock, Samba, Tango, Mango

Dentists

Dr. Iva Drill
and
Dr. Nova Kane

"Our Braces Go Places!"

- Caps, Hats, Crowns, Scepters, Bridges, Roads
- Root Canals, Branch Canals

"Where the Wait is Great"

Plenty of time to write that novel, make a kingsize quilt, or carve a lifesize statue of your pet rhino

Op T. Mist and Op T. Mum Opticians

All kinds of glasses:
rose-colored • juice • lemonade
Contact lenses • Bifocals • Tricycles

Landscape Capers

Backhoe Work • Forwardhoe work Top-Soil • Bottom Soil Trees, Shrubs, Grubs, Flubs Tree Pruning and Plumming

Mane Street Stables

Boarding • Trail Rides • Tack Shop • Nail Shop • Shoeing • Socking
A horse? Of course! phone 163-9573

What's the Good Word?

1. Which would you do with a new sweater, **wear** it or **ware** it?

2. To eat a banana, would you **peal** it or **peel** it?

3. What is another word for a commercial, an **add** or an **ad?**

4. If something is inexpensive, is it **cheap** or is it **cheep?**

5. Which is a huge ocean mammal, a **wail** or a **whale?**

6. If you're talking about the wind, would you say it **blew** or it **blue?**

7. Do you bake cookies using **flower** or **flour?**

8. When your arm hurts, are you in **pain** or in **pane?**

9. When you slice a pie, do you cut a **peace** or a **piece?**

10. Is a buzzing insect a **be** or is it a **bee?**

Answers on page 160

What's Wrong?

What Do You Know About ...?

Take a flying leap at this quiz. See if you can guess the correct answer to each question.

1. The "Stalder Shoot," the "Yamashita," and the "Diomidov" are
    A. locations for gymnastics competitions.
    B. moves named after gymnasts who invented them.
    C. restaurants where gymnasts eat healthy food.

2. Which of these is not a gymnastics event?
    A. freestyle
    B. rings
    C. balance beam

3. The parallel bars are
    A. made of steel.
    B. made of wood.
    C. made of aluminum.

4. In the floor exercise, a gymnast
    A. stays as near the center as possible.
    B. does all movements while lying on the floor.
    C. performs within a boundary.

5. In free exercises
    A. gymnasts do routines of their own choosing.
    B. the audience does not have to pay admission.
    C. birds are let out of cages at the beginning.

6. The horse apparatus was first used to
    A. teach trick riding to circus performers.
    B. keep children occupied at malls.
    C. train cavalry riders to mount quickly.

Answers on page 160

What Happened?

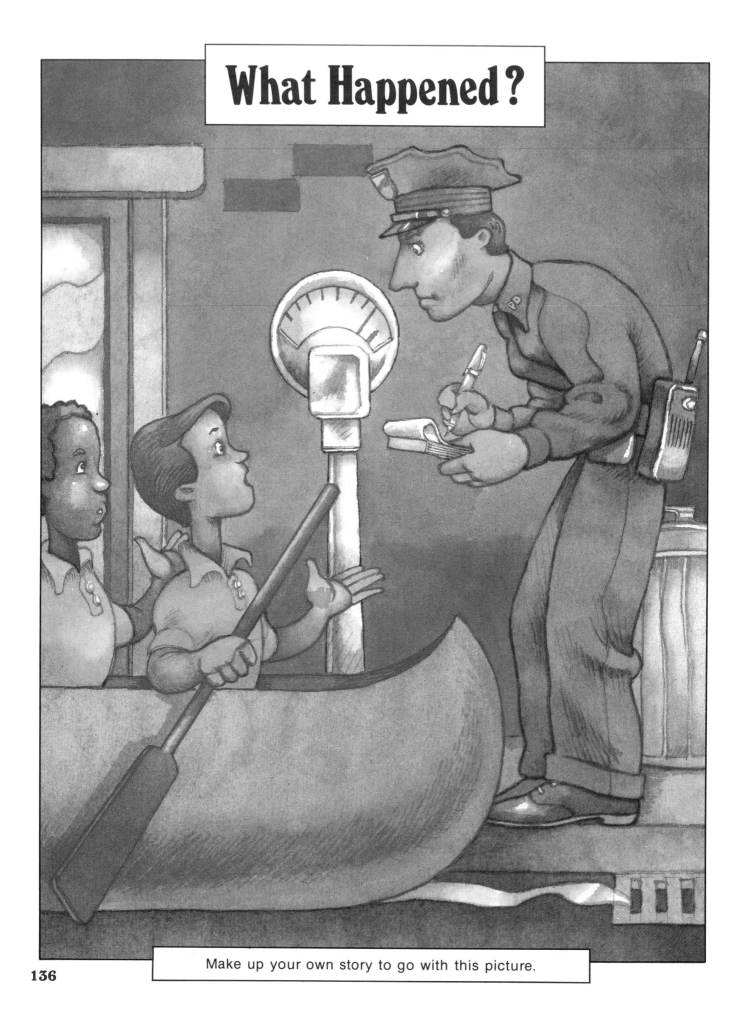

Make up your own story to go with this picture.

WHAT AM I?

How many of these holiday symbols
can you guess?

1. I have no eyes, nose, or mouth
until I meet something sharp.

2. Even when I'm not in the pink
people *love* my special shape.

3. You bake me to celebrate a number
one guy . . . and that's no lie!

4. You egg me on and keep on
hopping.

5. I'm always in a spin over this
holiday.

6. I stand straight and tall to show
off all my ribbons.

7. You want me to be really fresh so
I won't needle you.

8. The crowd oohs and ahhs until I
go out at night.

9. I have three leaves and am a
favorite of Irish people.

10. First I gobble, then you gobble.

Answers on page 160

What's Different?

There are at least 12 differences between these two pictures. How many can you find?

MARTIN FILCHOCK

Which Two Match?

Which two figures match?

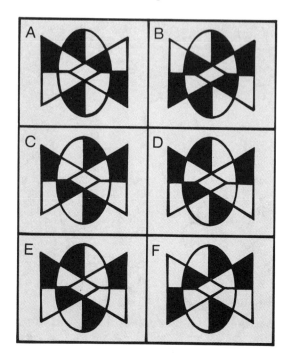

A B C D E F

What's So Funny?

1. If you have nine apples in one hand and ten in the other, what do you have?

2. What is a grape's mother's mother's mother called?

3. Why did the haunted house have such a big phone bill?

Answers on page 160

WHAT'S WRONG with these Pictures?

What's Wrong?

What's Next?

These pictures are out of order. For example,
E happened first, A second, and so forth. Can you
figure out the logical order for the rest?

Answers on page 160

WHAT'S WRONG with this Nursery Rhyme?

Humpty Dumpty sad on a wall,
Humpty Dumpty had a grey fall.
All the king's sauces,
And all the king's men,
Couldn't put Humpty to gather egg hen.

What's Wrong?

What Do You Know About ...?

1. Which of the following states is called the "Golden State" because it was once the site of plentiful gold deposits?
   - A. Montana
   - B. California
   - C. Florida

2. Which state is the home of the Grand Canyon, one of the Seven Natural Wonders of the World?
   - A. Arizona
   - B. New Mexico
   - C. Wyoming

3. Which state, known as the corn state, uses more land for farming than any other state?
   - A. Texas
   - B. Iowa
   - C. Georgia

4. Which of the following states is famous for its scenic beauty, produces more pecans than any other state, and has a capital named Salem?
   - A. Oregon
   - B. North Carolina
   - C. Kansas

5. Which state, known as the "Lone Star State," is the second largest of the 50 states and is best known for its large cattle ranches and vast oil fields?
   - A. Texas
   - B. Mississippi
   - C. Kentucky

6. Which state was the birthplace of eight United States presidents?
   - A. Tennessee
   - B. Maine
   - C. Virginia

Answers on page 160

WHAT'S WRONG?

Read these four comments about dinner at Aunt Bess's house. Then look at the pictures. Only one of the pictures shows the meal correctly. Can you figure out which one it is?

1. Aunt Bess makes the best cornbread I've ever had. Green vegetables are my favorite so I'm glad there were two kinds.

2. I had some of everything except the cranberry sauce because I'm allergic to cranberries. I had extra helpings of candied potatoes. It was delicious!

3. I love turkey with mashed potatoes and gravy. Everything was perfect but I ate too much pumpkin pie!

4. There's nothing I like better than green beans with mashed potatoes and gravy. Aunt Bess is a wonderful cook. Thinking about her dinner makes me hungry again!

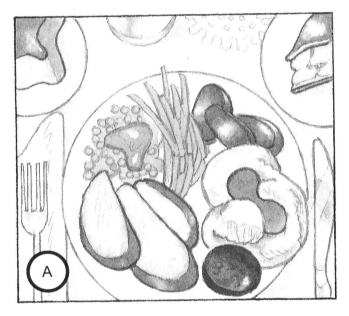

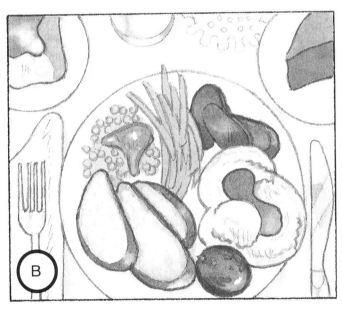

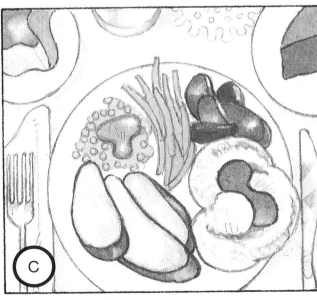

Answers on page 160

What's Alike?

Can you find 8 things that look the same in both of these pictures?

What's Wrong?

FISH

VALENTINE TREES

149

WHAT'S UP?

Tess closed her eyes and typed a sentence on her keyboard. Look at the keyboard and look at the sentence on the computer screen. Can you tell what mistake Tess made?

Yp ,slr yjod drmyrmvr

;ppl dp dytsmhr O kidy ,pbrf

,u gomhrtd pmr lru yp yjr

tohjy pg ejrtr yjru

str di((pdrf yp nr/

150

Answers on page 160

What's Out of Place?

In each set of four things, which one doesn't belong? Why not?

1. punt
   penalty
   pass
   putt

2. oxygen
   tin
   nitrogen
   helium

3. Columbia
   Germany
   Belgium
   Portugal

4. memory
   treble
   floppy
   cursor

5. mouse
   gerbil
   llama
   hamster

6. Tampa
   Lexington
   Orlando
   Miami

7. olive
   thyme
   cinnamon
   oregano

8. lasagne
   taco
   ravioli
   spaghetti

9. Macintosh
   Delicious
   Cabbage
   Jonathon

10. rectangle
    square
    triangle
    cone

11. pear
    lettuce
    spinach
    carrot

12. lobster
    cod
    clam
    shrimp

Answers on page 160

WHAT IS IT?

Can you tie these clues to the shapes that go with them?

1. Big squirt
2. It keeps Fido on line
3. Con-neck-tion
4. Long-distance link
5. It goes to waist
6. Wrist wrap
7. It goes to great lengths
8. Rod's need
9. It keeps you hopping
10. Water tow-er
11. Tennie tongue-tie

Answers on page 160

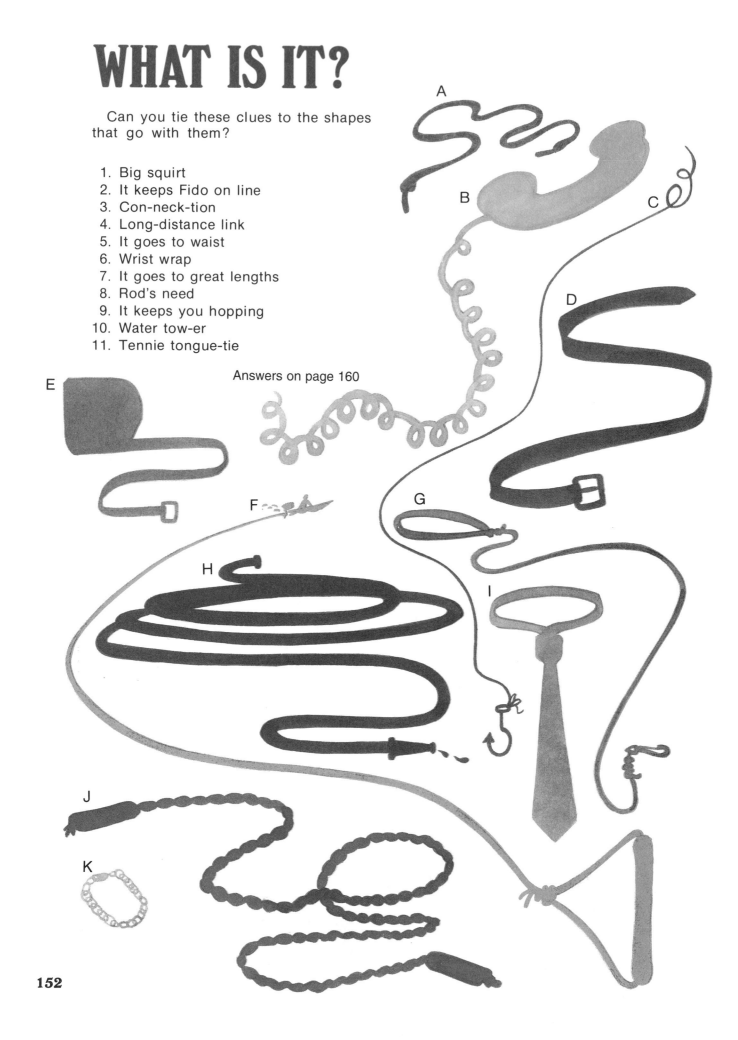

152

What's Different?

There are at least 10 differences between these two pictures. How many can you find?

MARTIN FILCHOCK

What's the Meaning of This?

Sometimes people say one thing when they mean another. See if you can guess the real meaning of each phrase below.

1. When your sister says sewing is her **cup of tea,** she really means . . .

    A. you are drinking her tea by mistake.
    B. she doesn't like coffee.
    C. she likes to sew a lot.

2. If your friend at school **let the cat out of the bag,** he most likely . . .

    A. accidentally told a secret.
    B. untied the laundry bag on the way to the vet's allowing the cat to get loose in your car.
    C. put the cat food away when you came home from the grocery store.

3. This morning you ate the **lion's share** of your breakfast. Did you . . .

    A. eat the part you were supposed to save for the lion at the nearby zoo?
    B. eat the biggest part of it?
    C. eat the bacon your mom was saving for your cat?

4. The school nurse tells you that you have **a frog in your throat.** Does she mean . . .

    A. your voice is hoarse?
    B. you swallowed your friend's pet?
    C. you can't sing very well?

5. When your uncle says your cousin really **took the bull by the horns,** he means . . .

    A. your cousin played the trumpet beautifully.
    B. he went into the neighbor's pasture and grabbed a bull by the ring in his nose.
    C. your cousin went right ahead and got the job done.

6. If your dad looks at you in your bedroom and says **"That's a pretty kettle of fish,"** he means . . .

    A. your aquarium is looking very pretty.
    B. you've gotten yourself into a big mess.
    C. your room looks like a bowl of fish chowder.

Answers on page 160

What's Your Number?

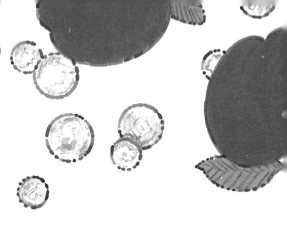

1. You are selling snacks at the school fair. A girl buys an apple for 35¢ and hands you a dollar bill. You have no quarters so you must make change using nickels and dimes only. How many different combinations of nickels and dimes could you use?

2. Look at these two pictures. If each teddy bear weighs one-half pound, how much does the doll weigh by itself?

3. How many of these circles are divided equally?

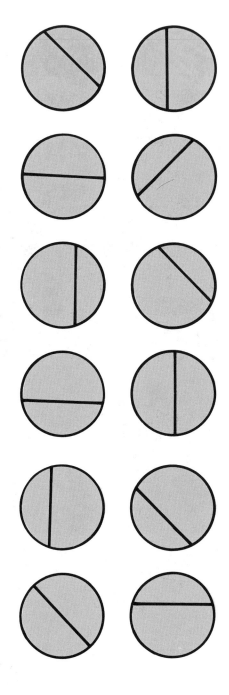

Answers on page 160

What's Different?

There are at least 10 differences between these two pictures. How many can you find?

Answers

You'll notice that answers are not provided for all pages. Some puzzles and activities are open-ended and designed for a broad range of age and skill levels. Getting the answer is not nearly as important as the thinking involved in finding an answer.

What's the Glitch? (page 3)
Tin rusts, so the Bi-Sea-Cle's frame would not last with underwater use.

What Rhymes? (page 5)
1. Mittens/Kittens
2. Dish/Fish
3. Log/Dog
4. Truck/Duck
5. Carrot/Parrot
6. House/Mouse

What Do You Know About Soccer? (page 7)
1. B. The goalie uses every part of the body to keep the ball out of the team's goal.
2. A. The World Cup tournament has been dominated by European and South American teams.
3. D. In the United States and Canada, football means something else, of course.
4. B. Each goal is worth one point, and the team with the most goals is the winner.
5. D. Hurdling is a track-and-field event. In soccer, dribbling means controlling the ball with your feet, passing means kicking the ball to a teammate, and marking means playing tight defense.

Who's Who? (page 7)
Susan—Jets
Craig—Panthers
Phillip—Hawks

What Am I? (page 10)
1. Penguin
2. Porcupine
3. Platypus
4. Panda
5. Parrot
6. Prairie dog
7. Porpoise
8. Panther

What's So Funny? (page 12)
1. A squid car
2. A mow hare
3. A lumber party
4. A catillac

What's Next? (page 14)
1. A
2. B
3. B
4. B
5. A
6. A

What Do You Know About Animals? (page 18)
1. B. Gibbons are tailless apes that live in Southeast Asia and the East Indies.
2. C. Termites are antlike insects that eat wood.

3. A. A tapir is a hoofed animal that lives in South America, Malaya, and Sumatra.
4. C. A spoonbill is a large wading bird that lives in the warm coastal regions of the world.
5. A. A chameleon is a lizard with the ability to change the color of its skin.
6. B. A skate is a ray with very large pectoral fins.

What's Up? (page 22)
March

What Is It? (page 24)
1. Scissors
2. Telephone
3. Candle
4. Fork
5. Dictionary
6. Door hinge

What's the Meaning of This? (page 26)
1. B   4. C
2. A   5. B
3. C   6. A

What's Your Number? (page 28)
A. 32
B. 9 2 7
   4 6 8
   5 10 3
C. 19
D. 2

What's the Big Idea? (page 30)
Each word includes the letters c-a-r: car, card, cardinal, carnation, carpenter, carpet, carrot, cart, carton, cartoon, cartwheel.

What's the Word? (page 31)
1. Made in the U.S.A.
2. I understand
3. Sliced bread
4. Three little pigs
5. Forever
6. Bulletin board
7. Drive-in movie
8. Simon says
9. Skyline
10. Antenna
11. Breakfast

What's the Glitch? (page 35)
After you've finished the **last** bite of the **last** muffin, there's still one bite left . . . Your ears could get frostbite!

What Goes with What? (page 37)
1. Arctic Circle
2. Egyptian pyramid
3. Telephone line
4. Ice cube
5. Baseball diamond

6. Times Square
7. Bermuda Triangle
8. Ice-cream cone

What Do You Know About Tennis? (page 39)
1. C. Love means a score of zero.
2. B. The serve is the way the ball is put into play.
3. B. Players must hit the ball over the net or lose a point.
4. A. The first player to win six games takes the set.
5. D. A double fault occurs when a player makes two bad serves in a row.

What's the Score? (page 39)
Brenda won the most games with nine wins. Kari won eight, Trina won four, and Sandy won two.

What Am I? (page 42)
Everest

Which Two Match? (page 44)
C

What's So Funny? (page 44)
1. Eggplant
2. She a-peeled to him, but Carrie didn't carrot all.
3. A beat beet.
4. "Lettuce get out of here!"

What's Next?
(page 46)
A-3   B-7   C-6
D-8   E-4   F-1
G-2   H-9   I-5

What Do You Know About Foreign Lands? (page 50)
1. The Taj Mahal is in India.
2. Portuguese is the language of Brazil.
3. The Danube River is in Europe.
4. Lasagna is more often associated with Italy.
5. Switzerland has no seacoast.
6. The mazurka is a Polish dance.

What's Up? (page 54)
Lizzie is a construction worker.

What Rhymes? (page 55)
My report is about currency, which is another word for **money**. Some currency is made of **metal**. In the United **States**, these **coins** are known as **pennies, nickels, dimes, quarters,** and **fifty-cent** pieces. We also have green **paper money** called **dollar bills. Money** is made at a place called a **mint**. It is controlled by the **Treasury** Department of our government. The government also makes rules for the **banks** where people save their **money**. My **mother** always says, "A **penny saved** is a **penny earned.**"

What Is It? (page 56)
1. Comb
2. Carrot
3. Hammer
4. Soup ladle
5. Fork
6. Baby rattle
7. Key
8. Teacup

What's the Meaning of This? (page 58)
1. B
2. C
3. A
4. C
5. A
6. B

What's Your Number? (page 60)
A. The beginning of your lucky number is 275; the final total is your secret!
B. Numbers 5 and 6 change places.
C. They each pick 24 apples.

$$106$$
$$-10$$
$$96 \div 4 = 24$$

What's the Big Idea? (page 62)
They can all be made from wood.

What's the Word? (page 63)
1. Bonnet
2. Centipede
3. Sign language
4. Discovered
5. Double check
6. Crossword
7. Merry-go-round
8. Two eggs over easy
9. Keep in touch
10. Leftover food

What's the Glitch? (page 67)
Underwater, sub dragging deflated balloon looks like really, really big jellyfish, thereby attracting really, really hungry sharks!

What's the Right Way Home? (page 69)
2

What Do You Know About Bicycles? (page 71)
1. B
2. C
3. A
4. C
5. B

Who Won? (page 71)
First Place: Lauren on the green bicycle.
Second Place: Doug on the yellow bicycle.
Third Place: Andrew on the orange bicycle.

Who Am I? (page 74)
Baseball player
Ballet dancer
Truck driver
Baker
Bank teller
Photographer

Which One Isn't Right? (page 76)
The sixth panel is numbered 7 instead of 6.

What's So Funny? (page 76)
1. A python (pie-thon)
2. A cold medal
3. March
4. The queen of clubs

What's Next? (page 78)
A-3   B-4
C-1   D-6
E-5   F-2

What Do You Know About Relatives? (page 82)
1. B   6. A
2. A   7. C
3. A   8. B
4. C   9. C
5. B   10. A

What's Up? (page 86)
Hector the hungry hound helped himself to the hot dogs. That's Hector hiding under the picnic table.

What's Out of Place? (page 87)
1. pumpkins (not grown on trees)
2. Ugly Duckling (not a nursery rhyme character)
3. Albuquerque (not a city in Texas)
4. pedal (not used by horseback riders)
5. racquet (not a musical instrument)
6. apple (not associated with Hawaii)
7. 25/2 (not equal to 50)
8. macaw (not a horse-like animal)
9. Alexander Hamilton (not a U.S. president)
10. dresser (not found in a kitchen)
11. flute (not a stringed instrument)
12. Seattle, Washington (not a state capital)

What Is It? (page 88)
1. gazebo
2. aglet
3. finial
4. cloak
5. tripod
6. cask
7. shrubbery
8. chariot
9. trellis
10. turret

What's the Meaning of This? (page 90)
1. B   4. B
2. A   5. C
3. C   6. B

What's Your Number? (page 92)
1. D
2. A-7
   B-8
   C-14
3. C
4. 11:51

What's the Big Idea? (page 94)
They are all used to measure things.

What's the Word? (page 95)
1. Nothing new under the sun
2. Narrow escape
3. Hole in one
4. Lemonade
5. Round off
6. Close call
7. Double-header
8. Countdown
9. Century
10. Sidewalk

What's the Glitch? (page 99)
You'll be in quite a **jam** if you don't clean up jelly-splattered walls! So your valuable playtime won't be **preserved** after all.

What's the Mix-Up? (page 101)
1. The large **ape** at the zoo frightened us.
2. The boy put the groceries in a paper **bag**.
3. Ida always puts a **lump** of sugar in her tea.
4. Jimmy says his dog is part **wolf**.
5. I hurt my **arm** when I threw the ball.
6. Ed and I are members of the swimming **team**.
7. Carol always walks at a fast **pace**.
8. The baby was taking a **nap** when we arrived.
9. I love to **read** the story of Cinderella.
10. Mother asked Sarah not to **gulp** her milk.
11. The bankleader bought a new **bugle**.
12. The beavers were busy building a **dam**.

What Do You Know About Basketball? (page 103)
1. A   3. C
2. B   4. A

What Am I? (page 106)
Poisen ivy

Who Has the Ball? (page 103)
Fred has the ball. From left to right the players are Ed, Ned, Fred, Ted, and Sylvester.

What's So Funny? (page 108)
1. Because it saw a horsefly.
2. Because they don't know how to knit.
3. Climb a tree and act like a nut.
4. At the farmacy (pharmacy).

Which Two Match? (page 108)
Panels 2 and 5 match.

What's Next? (page 110)
1-A   4-A
2-B   5-B
3-B   6-B

What Do You Know About States? (page 114)
1. A, C, D
2. A, B, C, E, F
3. A, C
4. B, C, D, E
5. A, B, C, E, F
6. A, C, D, E

What's Up? (page 118)
He is **not** a real astronaut. There are no plants on the Moon. Space suits couldn't be taken off because there is no air on the Moon. The astronauts couldn't drink from streams, because there is no water on the Moon. No vehicle was used for exploration of the Moon until the July, 1971, landing. That vehicle ran on electric batteries, not gas. Of the three astronauts who went to the Moon in July, 1969, two walked on the Moon's surface for about three hours.

What's Wrong with This Tale? (page 119)
1. There was an old woman who lived in a **shoe**.
2. Little Miss Muffet sat on a **tuffet**.
3. Cinderella lost her **glass slipper** at the ball.
4. When Pinocchio told lies, his **nose** grew and grew.
5. Rapunzel hung her **hair** out of the tower so the prince could climb up to her.
6. Everywhere that Mary went, her **lamb** was sure to go.
7. Snow White had **seven** friends who were dwarfs.
8. Dorothy went to see the Wizard of Oz, hoping he would help her get back to **Kansas**.
9. Sleeping Beauty awoke when the prince **kissed** her.
10. A **wolf** dressed up as Little Red Riding Hood's grandmother.

What Is It? (page 120)
1. sled runner
2. front of a toboggan
3. bicycle pedal
4. red wagon, where handle joins
5. ski pole end

What's the Meaning of This? (page 122)
1. B
2. B
3. A
4. B
5. C
6. A

What's Your Number? (page 124)
1. Each of the five special offers amounts to the same price per glass: 25 cents.
2. Twelve
3. Twenty-five times: once for each midnight plus twenty-three times in between.
4. Three of the pictures include a mistake.

What's the Big Idea? (page 126)
1. G
2. C
3. H
4. A
5. I
6. F
7. D
8. E
9. J
10. B

What's the Word? (page 127)
1. Fiddler crab
2. Quarter horse
3. Box turtle
4. Swordfish
5. Hammerhead shark
6. Firefly

What's The Glitch? (page 131)
If an ornery octopus happens to stroll by, he might think the pants are his!

What's The Word? (page 133)
1. wear
2. peel
3. ad
4. cheap
5. whale
6. blew
7. flour
8. pain
9. piece
10. bee

What Do You Know About Gymnastics? (page 135)
1. B
2. A
3. B
4. C
5. A
6. C

What Am I? (page 138)
1. Jack-'O-Lantern (Halloween)
2. Heart (Valentine's Day)
3. Cherry pie (Washington's Birthday)
4. Rabbit (Easter)
5. Dreidel (Hanukkah)
6. May pole (May Day)
7. Pine tree (Christmas)
8. Fireworks (Independence Day)
9. Shamrock (St. Patrick's Day)
10. Turkey (Thanksgiving)

Which Two Match? (page 140)
Figures D and E match.

What's So Funny? (page 140)
1. You have big hands.
2. She is called a grape grandma.
3. Someone was always calling ghost-to-ghost.

What's Next? (page 142)
A-2 B-5
C-6 D-4
E-1 F-3

What Do You Know About States? (page 146)
1. B
2. A
3. B
4. A
5. A
6. C

What's Wrong? (page 147)
C

What's Up? (page 150)
To make this sentence look so strange I just moved my fingers one key to the right of where they are supposed to be.

What's Out of Place? (page 151)
1. putt (not a football term)
2. tin (not a gas)
3. Colombia (not a European country)
4. treble (not a computer term)
5. llama (not a rodent)
6. Lexington (not a city in Florida)
7. olive (not a spice)
8. taco (not a type of pasta)
9. cabbage (not a type of apple)
10. cone (not a two-dimensional shape)
11. pear (not a vegetable)
12. cod (not a shellfish)

What Is It? (page 152)
1. H. garden hose
2. G. leash
3. I. necktie
4. B. phone card
5. D. belt
6. K. bracelet
7. E. tape measure
8. C. fishing line
9. J. jump rope
10. F. water ski tow rope
11. A. shoelace

What's the Meaning of This? (page 154)
1. C
2. A
3. B
4. A
5. C
6. B

What's Your Number? (page 156)
1. There are seven ways you could make change:
   Eleven nickels and one dime
   Nine nickels and two dimes
   Seven nickels and three dimes
   Five nickels and four dimes
   Three nickels and five dimes
   One nickel and six dimes
2. The doll weighs two pounds.
3. Three of the circles are divided equally.